SAINT JOHN'S UNIVERSITY PRESS

COLLEGEVILLE, MINNESOTA

SWIFT,
LORD,
YOU ARE
NOT

Kilian McDonnell, O.S.B.

Kilian McDonnell, OSB

"Matins," "The Monks of St. John's File in for Prayer,"
"Compline," "Fatima Ysif Bears a Son," "The Moment of
Decision," "The Call of Abraham," "Jonah's Flight," "Must
You Mumble?" "Pelagius Undone," "You Alone," "Perfection,
Perfection," "The Con," "Things I Dread," "The Younger
Son," "The Father of the Younger Son," "The Elder Son,"
"The Father of the Elder Son," "Lazarus Comes to Dinner,"
appeared originally in *The National Catholic Reporter*.
"The Death of My Mother" appeared in *America*. "From
Monastery to Cemetery: The Island of St. Michele, Venice,"
appeared in *The Benedictine Review*.

Library of Congress Control Number: 2003106839

ISBN 0-9740-9920-1

To the Memory of
Aimée and Patrick Butler
for their generosity
and vision

To the Board of Directors
of The Institute
for Ecumenical and
Cultural
Research for its
willingness
to carry on the vision

CONTENTS

IN THE

BEGINNING

WAS

THE WORD:

THE PROMISE

ADAM ON THE LAM

("They heard the Lord God walking in the garden
at the time of the evening breeze." Genesis 3:8)

In the cool of the evening we heard Yahweh
walking beneath the trees of Paradise,
the hush brushing the face searching
each broken twig, fallen leaf,
displaced stone. These friends do not betray me,
Adam on the lam—the dust still damp upon my limbs,
the breath of God still nostril-fresh, and shame
—quick and light—rests easily upon the ruddy
apple I did not choke to eat.
(I handle guilt extremely well.) I hear the voice
of sovereignty through the fall of forest shadows
"Adam, where are you?"

       I heard your scuffing sandals
upon the garden path, and I was afraid;
naked as I am, I hid myself.
"Adam, have you tasted of the tree in the middle
of the garden?"

"That cheeky woman you made
to be with me, she gave me and I ate,
but now I fear today is dying day,
as you decreed. And if the law in the sinews
of your name cannot be changed, can you mitigate
your unhurried oath: the day you eat, you die?"

"My statutes, sly son, you quote me to my face!
Could I adjust my word? I am God, not man,
mercy in your midst and that is law.
You will sweat thistles; the land will not give,
but you, spit and dirt in my image, shall live."

IN THE BEGINNING LAW

*("Of the tree of knowledge of good
and evil you shall not eat." Genesis 2:17)*

Seriously, do you really want
to start intimacy with a command?
Your first words, "Do not."

If we do, on that day we will die.
But she did, and so did I.
In the beginning finality, ultimacy.

We also hear, "Have sex and multiply."
Even embrace comes under edict.
You build gardens with a hammer.

The rabbis counted 365
"Thou shalt nots!"
248 "Thou shalts!" in the Law.

Clearly, a lot of pounding
to build safe carousels
in the damaged park downstairs.

After the bite we locate
ourselves in the universe with more
than academic mortarboards.

Somewhere in the apostolic succession
of sin and grace our thinning blood
found width in the narrows of your laws.

Could your law be unhectored liberty,
a superhighway with sign posts?
Are your mandates fallen mercies?

IN THE BEGINNING DYSFUNCTION?

(God created man in his image;
in the divine image he created him;
male and female he created them. Genesis 2:27)

It could not be!
Not possible!
Not Adam, uttering
the first of weasel words.

Not Eve, fondling
the apple before she
invents sin,
brings forth Cain,

who discovers murder.
In the beginning,
a dysfunctional family?
At the start, illusion?

God scrapes the ground
for dust. With clay
under his nails, he makes
an icon of himself, Adam,

one foot in the junk yard,
the other in the palace
of the king; and in the
rib, the threat of freedom.

If you cannot understand
the Sculptor, will the sculpted
make sense? If the Author
is beyond you, will you

comprehend the book?
Beyond telling: the Untouchable
leaves his marrow in
the bones that will dance.

CAIN: SIN CROUCHES AT MY DOOR

("And the Lord had regard for Abel and his offering,
but for Cain and his offering
he had no regard." Genesis 4:4-5)

Unstable, unfair,
capricious is the one
who writes the rules,
flaunts them.
How to live on Yahweh's slippery terms,
which smell of snake oil.

Promises, promises,
still God shuns
my sacrifice,
no reason given,
but the fatty meat of Abel's offering
rises like incense to the heights.

For lumpy brother,
his nothingness yet,
God thieves
my birthright;
himself, the second born,
is chosen.

Sin crouches at my door
and I slay him.

Though blood cries from the ground,
my changeling God does not scorn
to place upon my freedom
a sheltering mark,
lest any raise a hand against me,
as I till the earth
—which does not yield its strength—
caught between God's decrees,
my decisions
and the night.

THE CALL OF ABRAHAM

("Now the Lord said to Abram,
'Go from your country.'" Genesis 12:1)

Talk about imperious.
Without a "may I presume?"
No previous contact,
no letter of introduction,
this unknown God
issues edicts.

This is not a conversation.
Am I a nobody
to receive decrees
from one whose name
I do not know?

I have worshipped my own god.
To you I had addressed no prayers,
but quick,
like sudden fire in the desert,
I hear "Go."

At seventy-five,
am I supposed to scuttle my life,
take that ancient wasteland, Sarai,
place my arthritic bones

upon the road
to some mumbled nowhere?

Let me get this straight.
I will be brief.
I summarize.

In ten generations since the Flood
you have spoken to no one.
Now, like thunder on a clear day,
you give commands:
pull up my tent,
desert the graves of my ancestors,
leave Haran
for a country you do not name,
there to be a stranger.

God of the wilderness,
from two desiccated lumps,
from two parched prunes,
you promise all peoples of the earth
will be blessed in me.

You come late, Lord, very late,
but my camels leave in the morning.

ISHMAEL MIDWAY

("He shall be a wild ass of a man." Genesis 16:12)

Conceived on the tolerated blanket of Hagar,
—from the start a tacky compromise—
because dry-gulched Sara could not,
and Father,
no matter what the calendar,
must have a son;
so hectored into heat,
goosed into passion,
the man of faith,
though enfeebled by his years,
embraced the lippy slave,
and behold here I am,
a wild untethered ass at war with all;
I stand alone outside the clan,
beyond the promise,
an in-between,
a halfway sort of lad am I,

not elected,
not rejected
—betwixt am I—
but this my brag:
Yahweh's care is not unshared;
Isaac has no lock on benedictions.
God bends over my muddled blood.
Though begot on a different spread,
outside the covenant,
I receive a blessing,
junior size.

MOSES: THE COST OF DOUBTING

("You shall not cross over." Deuteronomy 34:4)

Lord of Israel and skies
Please consider who I am.
Face to face, eyes to eyes
we spoke, I and I-who-am.

Now you say, "Here you die."
Cries, remorse and blood of beasts
till the moon fails, priests faint.
Nothing can undo; nothing satisfies.

Joseph's bones will rest there,
lie honored in the land.
Which generic mound of sand
will mark my grave in nowhere?

One measly doubt can undo
all fidelity, one wary
hesitation, a single weary,
scrawny disbelief blew

forty years of pain? My sin
rolls down Mount Nebo like thunder
muffling Sinai's noisy pact.
Note: Torah and Mercy are kin.

"You shall not enter in, no.
Speak no more, you shall not go."

AS ADAM KNEW EVE

("Should anyone be scandalized
that we have taken the words
'Adam knew his wife' as an example
of the knowledge of God?" Origen)

Of course, I'm scandalized
that I should know my God
as Adam knew his wife.
—two in one flesh—

This talk of the little bed,
kisses on the mouth,
love richer than wine,
a young stag on the prowl,

standing behind the wall,
looking through the lattices
calling "the winter is past,
Now is time for love.

Hurry, hurry!
Arise, my lovely,
let me see your face.
Come away with me."

Do not stir up love
until it is ready
to last longer than malice.
The flesh is forever.

THE DEATH OF MOSES: A MIDRASH

The Angel of Death could no way prevail,
could not possess his ancient soul,
Moses was adamant. He would not go.
He had histories to write, laws to give.

"Already you have made too many words,"
the Lord had said to Moses, Giver of the Law.
"Now, Gabriel, my warrior in charge
of paradise, go and fetch him home."

"But Yahweh Lord, how could I presume
to snatch the soul which weighs much more
than sixty legions of ordinary spirits?
This, Lord, is beyond an angel's strength.

Then Yahweh said to Michael, the prince of all
the angels, he, one who is like God, opening up
the gates of heaven, "You go and bring him in."
With tears he pleads release from such audacity.

Then Satan asked for leave to collect the man.
Girding himself with great cruelty,
wrapping himself in wrath and rage
he came upon Moses writing the Unsayable Name,

its splendor sunning through the prophet's face.
"Begone, I will not give my soul to you."
But die he must upon the mountain—and now.
So God himself descends to do the death.

With Gabriel God spreads the sheets upon
the bed, God smooths the softness of the pillow flat,
and lays the old man down,
the Lord covering him in quilted purple.

Then bending over, God kisses Moses
upon the mouth, and sucks his soul to himself.
Yahweh and the angels weep for Moses,
they dig a valley grave and bury him,

where no one knows.

JONAH'S FLIGHT

("Jonah set out to flee to Tarshish
from the presence of the Lord." Jonah 1:3)

Off he flees in the opposite direction
of Nineveh, away from all those bacchic
Assyrians, who might repent at God's word,
away from my presence, away from his call.

I, Yahweh, hat in hand, hear "No,
I will not go to Nineveh to preach
salvation from their ziggurats,
where incense is offered to Ishtar."

Stomping righteous feet, he bitches toward Joppa,
"Yet now Nineveh, totem to blood,
whose shame stands naked before your face?
I, bring your nettled Word? Fat chance!

I pay my desperation fare, leave
behind his Lordship, land, and temple court.
His presence violates the boundaries
of geography, pursues me on the sea."

Quit of Yahweh he would be in Tarshish?
I, who invented chaos theory,
stretched out the heavens, shut in the upper waters,
laid the deep foundations of the earth,

and he would cup me in his hand, teach me wisdom,
put commands between my teeth, build walls and borders
for my mercies. Tell me, you who are wise and
    have knowledge,
why am I lumbered with this frazzling prophet?

So I have the sailors suicide him
into the sea, swallowed into the stomach
of my servant whale, who finds the prickly ballast
brings on indigestion. That speaks to me.

For three days and three nights Jonah
was in the dyspeptic beast, rumbling among
the odds and ends of last night's supper,
then belched onto the port of his departing.

MUST YOU MUMBLE?

("Then the Lord came and stood there calling
'Samuel, Samuel.'" 1 Samuel 3:10)

Speak, Lord, your servant listens.
Now, how about a straight word?

No more Ezekiel prophecies,
wheels within wheels.

It is not enough to drag
the hem of your garment

in the sand of Miami's beach
so I can read its scratchings.

Though I'm a Minnesota groundling,
I do not need the clarity

of Greek necessity. But no more
shadows on the cavern walls.

You are always turning off the lights,
blowing out the single candle.

Please, no more muttering
in your beer, like some dark Luther,

caught between the impossibilities
of Law and the freedom of the Gospel.

I just need some stay
against the cosmic dust

as I drag the bag of my illusions
along the street of my ineptitude.

Try a little logic on the universe.
Steady, please, Oh God of iron whim.

I ask no Mount Sinais, no Tabors,
no cloud by day, no fire by night,

just one unambiguous touch
lasting one beat of my heart.

PELAGIUS UNDONE

("You have accomplished for us all we have done."
Isaiah 26:12)

No sudden Tabors,
    No angelic visitations
        Betrayals had not reached
        a critical mass.

My fig leaf
    had not fallen off.
        My sins had not been published
        in the *Morning Mirror.*

But after years of "light off,"
    as I turned to hang
        my jacket on the wall
        a "light on" moment.

Stupid groundings
    were my own;
        I had chosen
        all the ports.

But there is a management,
    like wildest love,
        that leaves me free,
        opens wide the gate.

IMPATIENCE AT THE LOOM

("You cut me from the loom." Isaiah 38:12)

Like a weaver you roll up my life,
while thread is left upon the spool,
before half my days are counted,
unfinished, you cut it from the loom.
My years are still before me.
China is not yet visited.

All my joys are children still,
and my games have only started.
Tongues I have not spoken,
windows I have not looked through,
loves I will never meet.
Now you blow the whistle?

You roll up my life like a weaver,
you cut it from the loom,
unfinished
at five and eighty.
China is not yet visited,
China is not yet visited.

YOU ALONE

("You are my God.
My happiness lies in you alone." Psalm 16:2)

You've become accustomed to our lies,
the pious blasphemies we utter
on our knees, worthy of David,
fresh from Bathsheba's bed,
ready to send Uriah to the front,
the letter in his hand.

But what if we had only truths
to tell, if only transparencies to show,
no Hittite offering
to cover up the void.
Are our dysfunctional truths
more endurable than squeaky fibs?

So thank God for sturdy frauds,
for Davids—easy on the ethics—
who know the vacancies within,
who limp—but oh!—with style, brocading
golden glories out of the trash heap of the heart,
hoping the Lord God does not wince.

DON'T LOOK TOO CAREFULLY

("O search me God and know my heart." Psalm 39:23)

What sudden senile arrogance
provoked this bid to despair?

If you knock, God, be prepared
to see what stands behind the door:

unswept floors, unmade
beds, unwashed dishes

in the sink, a lone Giotto
unhung against the wall.

(I, too, have been to the Uffizi,
read Dostoevski, Yeats.)

If you turn over a stone
on my beach, what creatures scurry.

Dig in my ruins, you sift
buried rags of intent.

Uproot my elm, you pull up
forgotten teen-age tinsel.

Poke my cinders, you stir
fires best unremembered.

Search me not, test
no more. Take me as I am.

THEN IT IS FINISHED, DONE?

("He will judge the world . . . with his truth." Psalm 96:13)

Did I hear correctly? You said truth?
    You bore me up on eagle wings,
        and now it has come to truth?

If you stoop to searching hearts,
    who will defend me from my lies?
        Do you really want my blood?

Truth gives no quarters,
    takes no prisoners.
        All have turned aside.

Truth is the length of the unforgiving
    rope as my tattered life
        falls through the trap door.

All our truths need
    bungee cords, the Nicodemus
        night, the side door in.

Even in God, truth
    is not pure. Seduced by mercy,
        ravished at the door by compassion.

THE CON

("For your name's sake, O Lord,
save me." Psalm 143:11)

My days are few in number,
full of trouble and sin.

I have smudged my single copybook,
the erasures all show through.

When I decorously cover the deletions
with fig leaves, they wilt.

If you count all iniquities,
Lord, who will stand?

Must you really insist
on your plan A?

Already I have set out
on my plan B.

Adjust to my facts,
wink, and let me in.

I could give a thousand sterling
reasons why you should,

all of them shabby, shopworn.
A weary God might consider.

But think not of me.
For your sake, save me.

UNKEPT PROMISES

("I have more understanding than
all my teachers." Psalm 118:99)

Promises were made:
You would be my guide.

I would never lose the map.
The light would always burn.

I would know more
than all my teachers.

Then why do you use
clicks for words,

speaking opaque riddles,
like the ancient Hebrews

writing backwards,
using only consonants?

Why do I see only
your backsides—and in the dark?

You cut deep.
To staunch the flow

of blood you hand me
a styptic pencil.

You break me.
Like Van Gogh, I need

twenty-four self portraits
to remember who I am.

You sprinkle clods
of earth on my casket

with that irrevocable thud.
But to whom shall I go?

Who has life
no one deletes?

NOWHERE TO HIDE

("Whither shall I flee from your presence?" Psalm 138:8)

You've had your claws in me,
You've read my bloodless heart,
rummaged through my stumblings East,
numbered all my lurchings West.

You search the path before me.
My lying down you know
before I find my bed,
before I rest my head.

While the word is still upon my lips,
you've heard it all before.
You compass me behind,
ahead you set your traps.

If I climb the sky,
your might awaits me at the door.
If I descend below,
your glory hears me on the stairs.

Escape? Who said escape?
If I couch in hell,
your Spirit's prints
are burnt upon the sands.

If I search where none can go,
if I seek undiscovered planets,
there in the folds of silence
your face looks out.
And if I say the dark
will hide my eyes from you,
your black will dazzle
out the night,

unshield the lamp you are.
No more dark upon the land.
Your mercy holds me fast;
Your compassion pins me to the floor.

—But you leave me free—
Too great this knowledge, Lord,
Too high,
too wide.

SWIFT, LORD, YOU ARE NOT

("*Quickly God causes his blessing to flourish.*" Sirach 11:22)

This is not my experience.
You are not God at the ready.

After you set off the big bang
you invented light years, dawdling.

Dispatch you dropped down
the nearest black hole.

After the pyrotechnics of the start
you looked away, sabbathed.

When I think you are raising your arm
to stretch it out like Moses

so I can prevail over the Amalekites,
it is biblical sleight of hand.

Actually, you're raising your arm
to fix an arrow on your bow

aimed at some interstellar gases,
storms on the sun.

Think less of galaxies.
Think small.

Then, without the heavy equipment,
stoop and hasten to help me.

THINGS I DREAD

("The fear of the Lord is the beginning of wisdom." Proverbs 1:7)

Lifting the edge of the blanket
they will see my unwashed feet.
God has a photographic memory.
The dragon at the gate does not sleep.

Climbing the North face of Everest.
The shadow wolves are not a mirage.
Before the end the road just stops.
And, most of all, I fail at dying.

To be honest, all these I can manage,
though it is one damn bother.
But the ultimate terror: I will be measured
with the measure I measured out.

PERFECTION, PERFECTION

("I will walk the way of perfection." Psalm 101:2)

I have had it with perfection.
I have packed my bags,
I am out of here.
Gone.

As certain as rain
will make you wet,
perfection will do you
in.

It droppeth not as dew
upon the summer grass
to give liberty and green
joy.

Perfection straineth out
the quality of mercy,
withers rapture at its
birth.

Before the battle is half begun,
cold probity thinks
it can't be won, concedes the
war.

I've handed in my notice,
given back my keys,
signed my severance check, I
quit.

Hints I could have taken:
Even the perfect chiseled form of
Michelangelo's radiant David
squints,

the Venus de Milo
has no arms,
the Liberty Bell is
cracked.

THE BEGGAR'S QUESTION

("The Lord is my light and my salvation,
of whom should I be afraid." Psalm 27:1)

When I am attacked,
You are my fortress.

When I look for shelter,
You are my refuge.

When I stumble,
Your arm is my support.

When I am cold,
You are my fire.

When I die
You are my resurrection.

You swear
by your holiness.

Then why this vacancy
in my footsteps?

IN THE BEGINNING

WAS

THE WORD:

FULFILLMENT

THE YOUNGER SON

("*So he set off and went to his father.*" Luke 15:18)

The gold is gone, and the last
    tubercular floozy has stamped
      her foot, swished an angry
        skirt, and slammed the door.

In pursuit of the rapture of the deep
    I settled for giggles in the back room.
    A comedian with no more jokes
      stumbling off stage left.

Shame can wait, not hunger.
    I remember the mutton, the dates,
      uneaten in my father's pantry,
        and not a single sow in sight.

How hunger teaches the strategies
    of guilt; the husks of swine
      are wise if you will listen.
        Famine is seeing, unveiling.

Perhaps he would take me back
    if I chose the right words.
      "At eighteen, Father, I asked
        for mine, though you lived.

You gave the portion due me,
  full freedom for the road.
    And I was gone for years
      of tavern geniuses and tattoos.

The stomach remembers the stories
  of lost things: drachmas
    swept from under the bed,
      sheep freed from the brambles.

Remembrance always has a twin,
  like the mirror on the wall which speaks.
    Why not a son who was dead,
      startled into life by memory."

THE FATHER
OF THE YOUNGER SON

("While he was still far off his father saw him." Luke 15:20)

Even after I gave up
keeping the tiger cub
in his cage, I picked it up,
forgetting snarls and claws,
though I have bite marks,

scratches, to show love
comes late, scarred to wisdom.
Though you protect the cub
from larger cats, beware.
Young tigers have no shame.

The years I do not count
that I have passed the window in the front
searching the road for a sign
of that tiger no leash could check,
unmuzzled, free, and bleeding.

The helpless ache is ordinary,
the Thursday tedious, as I give a
passing glance through the window
at the dot on the far horizon
walking as many have walked before.

But the way he swings his arms,
turns his head, slightly
pigeon-toed. I am out the door,
down the stairs, down the road,
running, arms outstretched.

My embrace, my tears, my laughter
gather in all the years,
my kiss stops rehearsed
genealogies of sin, outlawing of self.
Of course, you are my son.

Be quick, steward, clothe him
as befits the son of a king,
the best robe from my chest,
goose the cook, load
the table with meats and wines.

call in friends and foes,
blaze the night into day
with torches, push the chairs
against the wall, pluck the harps,
strike the largest timbrel.

When the dead come back you drink.
When the lost are found you dance.

THE ELDER SON

(The elder son refuses to enter the house:
"You have never given me even a young goat
so that I might celebrate with my friends." Luke 15:29)

So he's back, Stud the Magnificent,
    himself, him whom you love.
You put rings on his fingers,
    cloak him in silk, kill
the grain-fed calf, call
    in the flutes so he nights
away the defiances of day,
    dances deceit to your tambourines.

Himself brings only pain.
    And you could not wait to be deceived.
You expect it, bow beneath
    the blow. Yet again. And you weep.
This idiocy of love is tacky.

I fetch and carry;
    I wait to be chosen,
reschedule my life for you.
    No coat of many colors,

no gold for my fingers,
   no sandals for my feet,
no fatted calf to bleed for me,
   no harp to pluck for joy.
This son has yet to dance with friends
   around a pot of goat stew.

Him you have loved, him.
No, I will not come in.

THE FATHER OF THE ELDER SON

("But we had to celebrate." Luke 15:32)

Son, you are always with me.
    All my pastures, granges, granaries,
all are yours, have ever been.
    You know you are my very self.
But for the living owner
    I did not blow the ramshorn.

You are right, of course:
    my love is tacky, untidy.
But you mistake to balance love,
    to measure it by level tablespoons,
like a chemist weighing arsenic.
    no excess.—You were never dead.

When the grave throws up a son
    there is a commotion of love,
a proper father malady,
    like a three-alarm riot in the heart.
We dance, we sing, we lift
    our cups, because we must.

Now I blow the ramshorn.

BROKEN TILE AND ROOF REPAIR

("When they could not bring him to Jesus because
of the crowd, they removed the roof . . ." Mark 2:4)

Given the high cost of roof repair
these days, and the expense of broken tile,
surely the Master would protest, as they tear
away the ceiling boards to drop me, while
below, where no room is, himself makes space
for the pushy paralytic in the house
of friends. Me, the image of God straight
from the back alley, my life wiped clean
for public grace with late remorse, fresh
from faith, slightly hyped to rouse a reluctant
Lord, and, if pressed, to bait the country Healer
with the grand entrance hard to top. He spread
his hands to touch me free. "Blasphemy" they said.

IN THE KITCHEN

("In the sixth month the angel Gabriel . . . ." Luke 1:26)

Bellini has it wrong.
I was not kneeling
on my satin cushion
quietly at prayer,
head slightly bent.

Painters always
skew the scene,
as though my life
were wrapped in silks,
in temple smells.

Actually I had just
come back from the well,
placing the pitcher on the table
I bumped against the edge,
spilling water on the floor.

As I bent to wipe
it up, there was a light
against the kitchen wall
as though someone had opened
the door to the sun.

Rag in hand,
hair across my face,
I turned to see
who was entering,
unannounced, unasked.

All I saw
was light, white
against the timbers.
I heard a voice
I had never heard.

I heard a greeting,
I was elected,
the Lord was with me,
I pushed back my hair,
stood afraid.

Someone closed the door.
And I dropped the rag.

THE FAMILY TREE

*("And Judah begot Perez and Zerah by Tamar . . ."
Matthew 1:3)*

The truth is in the blood, they say.
Blood lines tell no lies.
What is written there is written;
no sly erasures, no dodges in the dark.

Matthew kept his tax records,
knew who had paid, who still owed,
what to Caesar, what to God;
knew not to falsify his book.

When he made lists of begots,
traced the blood of Jesus,
he kept the shame they had recited
on nights around the Galilean fires.

Twice-spurned Tamar, once Judah's
whore during sheepshearing beside
the road to Bethlehem, his signet
a pledge on future payment.

Rahab, the harlot, built
her house into the city wall
for ease of egress, betrayed
her king, a cord her guarantee.

Bathsheba, wife of Uriah, David
bedded quickly, quicker dispatched
hubby to the front, letter
in his helmet, Bathsheba willing.

Solomon, triumphant in his riddles,
glorious in his temple, wise
in his palaces, dumb dumb
in his thousand wives and concubines.

The roots of his tree are here.
Bloods speaks to blood,
no lie is found in it.
The purging is from within the flow.

THIS NIGHT A CHILD IS BORN

(To David: *"Your throne shall be established forever."*
2 Samuel 7:16)

To the plucker of strings,
slayer of Goliath,
the whole of Palestine,
with fixed borders,
a chain of fortified cities.
The bridle taken out
of the Philistine's hands.
The Ark in Jerusalem.

Yahweh swore
David's dynasty
would rule forever.
By a perpetual covenant
his seed would sit
upon the throne.
The gold of the nations
would flow to Zion.
Kings would kneel.

But the scribe's indigo
ink was not dry

on the Acts of Solomon,
in the Chronicles of Israel,
when Jeroboam cried,
"To your Tents, O Israel,"
tearing the kingdom,
scattering the pieces.
Perpetuity crashed.

The priests still sang
over the ruins of Zion:
"By the word of the Lord
the heavens were made.
The Lord decides
the number of the stars,
calls each by its name.
The word cannot fail;
it stands forever."

Tonight Word
becomes history.
The seed of David
sits upon his throne,
a kingdom without fixed
borders. Kings kneel,
bringing gold,
frankincense and myrrh.
His reign is forever.

THE VISITATION

*("For as soon as I heard the sound of your greeting,
the child in my womb leaped for joy." Luke 1:44)*

To speak my word
I cannot wait
for break of water,
birth stool.

I have not tasted locusts,
nor wild honey;
no desert sands
beneath my feet.

Understand! three months
before I kick
my way out I know
Light when I see it.

Like David dancing
and tumbling before
the Ark of the Lord
with all his might,

I leap against
the womb, waltz
delight against
the cord too short.

Before this lump of life,
this whiff of blood
already noisy,
I am less than frailty.

I know who goes
into the hill country,
stands before the door.
I know. I know.

LAZARUS COMES TO DINNER

("They gave a dinner for him, Lazarus was one of them
at table with him." John 12:2)

Of course, I'm an oddity,
Not another one around.
I've been there and back,
and what's more, I stank.

When I attend a banquet,
they come. No no-shows,
no compelling them to enter,
no one without a wedding garment.

Talk about a conversation piece.
Sidelong glances
as I break a crust of bread
—had he taken tea with angels?—

I raise my glass of wine,
and they nudge their neighbors
—can he be thirsty, who drank
from the ultimate barrel?—

I speak to the Master about
the price of barley—do they share
memories from the cave that would
stupefy the mountains?—

OK, I have smudged the clear
edges of reality, broken
the quantum barrier? Only this
I say: truth is a moving target.

GUESS WHO'S COMING TO DINNER?

*("He said to Simon: . . . You gave me no kiss; but from the time
she came in she has not stopped kissing my feet." Luke 7:45)*

Overly dressed desire,
a paradise in skirts swishes
past the parched rectitude
of Simon to pour alabastered
oil and tears on his feet
there among the dinner guests.

Purchased beds and a denarius
for red lips, when broken,
see in the night what
sterilized prayer shawls,
properly adjusted, miss
in the glare of high noon.

Wholesale kisses on the stairs,
bought embraces in the back room
she cashed in for free love,
crashing Simon's party,
spreading her hair in cascades
to dry the Master's feet.

Simon is already forgotten.
She is with the ultimate lover.

A MANUAL FOR CLIMBERS

("The love of God has been poured into our hearts through the Holy Spirit that has been given to us." Romans 5:5)

Surely, this is right.
One begins at the bottom,
like ascending the ladder
to conquer the fire.

One foot up, then the other.
No parachutes to the top,
no express elevator.
The faint need not apply.

God wrestled with primeval
darkness in the waters
of chaos. After seven days,
God rested. Not I.

To build muscle
I keep pumping iron.
If I stop to breathe,
I am back at the bottom.

After decades of climbing
I'm still on ground floor.
I had it all wrong.
You start at the top.

MARY MAGDALENE THE APOSTLE

("Go to my brothers and tell them . . ." John 20:17)

Not promising,
not a good beginning,
to send Mary with the news
before the day is bright.

Had the hand he laid on her
killed the whiff
of seven demons
he had exorcised?

Anyway, by law
not to be trusted.
As witness,
very dubious.

Why had he appeared,
first of all, to her?
Why make trouble now?
Not street smart!

She walks the garden path
while it is dark,
the fortress of Antonia still
threatening the small of the night,

sees angels in white
guarding an empty space,
and turns to find the gardener,
(fretting over trampled cabbages?)

who is dumb before her question,
but says her name,
and, in the speaking,
suddenly it is dawn.

She reaches out a hand
to touch the yesterday,
and grasps the feet of all
the untouchable tomorrows.

She who loiters finds,
sent to tell the others
before the history is cooked,
and served on silver platters.

But the huddled guardians
of despair will not eat.
The report of glory from a woman?
Not street smart!

MIRROR,
MIRROR ON THE WALL

("Who are you to argue with God?" Romans 9:20)

Can you spare a moment?
A crooked cucumber
I am not. I am you
lower case.

If the original is misty,
a clear copy not likely.
You have answers!
I've got questions.

Potter, tell me this!
Why do your vessels
come from the turning wheel
having no handles?

Even you have problems.
Where does my freedom
to spill break
your mastering arm?

ALONG

THE

CLOISTER WALK

GRAMMATICA ARTIUM

(For Doris Caesar's Statue of John the Baptist)

The children and Agnes Ramler
gather around the sunken baptistery
beneath the black Baptist
guarding the waters of life.

He towers vatic, angular.
Had a drunken God forgotten
curves? Or unstable matter
too soon hardened into lumps?

An accusing neck, like the unfinished
cliffs of Everest. Hollow
eyes watching the doors
of eternity slam shut.

A leather strip girds
the camel's hair around the loins
barely fed with locusts
and wild honey from cactus.

A stray from the wrath of God
preparing the threshing floor
for the burning of the chaff, the gathering
of good wheat into granaries.

The youngest: "Why the dirty
bathing suit? Why is John
so ugly?" Agnes offers:
"Dat's where de art comes in."

KILIAN DOES NOT HAVE
ENOUGH TO DO

("What induced you to write poetry
after you came to prison? You never
composed any poems before." Cebes and Evenus
question Socrates in prison. Plato, Phaedo)

In my monastery
an old monk said:
"Kilian does not have
enough to do.
He writes poetry."

Not enough to do?
But, brother dear,
holy Socrates,
just before he took
the cup of hemlock,

began to write
poetry for Apollo.
No verse ever came
from his quill before
his prison days.

Those last hours,
before the poison
crept cold
down his legs,
he turned to poetry.

Not to while away
the hours, but to
scrub his soul.
Conscience made
him write his hymns.

We live in the hollow
of the earth, in a cave.
We cannot read the story
on the pages of the surface,
climb its Tabors.

In the deep cave
we see only shadows
cast upon the wall,
images reflected from above.
What do we know?

Poetry is groping
in the highest hollow
of the cavern, giving
body to the blurs
our fingers seem to touch.

Poetry is for dying.
Not for making arguments,
but for stories of the surface,
preparing for one's Apollo.
Not enough to do?

NURSING HOME CHAPEL

God lives down the corridor,
last door on the left.
At nine I bring the wine
pressed from the defiant grapes
of five and eighty years.
For bread, the mud cakes of my days,
carefully burnt in the sun.
The wheelchair cannot strut,
and the brag is gone,
but these gifts
I lay upon the altar
and see God bending over
my small mess
with infinite delight.

DORIS CAESAR'S STATUE
OF MARY IN THE GARDEN

I do not like you here,
unhoused, exiled
from the monastery church,
like a dotty aunt
one hides in the closet
when company comes.

The cheeky, merciless
students dubbed you
"Our Lady of the Brassiere"
because you're busty.
Are all virgins
flat-chested?

We dismissed you to the furthest
cove of the garden,
hidden by two oaks,
to shield from the shock
of seeing a woman
with breasts too suddenly.

At your shoeless feet
the run off water
from the center fountain,
a mini-Mississippi,
to console you
in this corner of nowhere.

Not for public viewing,
this night virgin
in warrior bronze,
a neck of astonishment,
great Hebraic eyes,
seeing what cannot be seen.

Strong as an army
in battle array.
In your hand a branch
of budding life,
an arm lifted
to fend off the wonder

of the word you hear
dug from canyons
of the strictly preposterous:
Power will fall.
You will bear
God with skin.

Dark Lady,
Do not stay here.
Step down from your pedestal
(watch the stones upon the path)
and take your public place
with your breasts unbound.

STRIPPING THE ALTAR

(Paul Schwietz, O.S.B., 47, Monk/Forester. May 4, 2000)

Unscheduled, the valve just stopped.
Technology turned sullen,
choked off the blood,

as though high on the banner
the giant Trinity bell
in full swing cracked,

flinging a strangled noise
above the blooming cherries
Maying the Watab Lake,

startling a solitary heron,
sending it lifting, pumping
low across the waters.

His driver's license opens
Paul's Body Shop, at the ready,
with parts to ship.

They harvest an arm for the bone bank,
liver for a nameless lad,
lungs on call.

The body broken into pieces,
given up for others, passed around,
with fragments left over,

the altar stripped to the stone,
bare, rough to the touch,
ready for the spilling of the blood.

Too soon the oak trees drop their leaves,
the savanna chants the Requiem,
the wetlands weep.

Wheat dying upon the ground,
grapes twice crushed,
fire the prairie.

MY FUNERAL

Brother Gregory
takes pride
in his caskets: no silks,
no satin quiltings,
no pillowed linings,
inlaid arabesques are absent,
just the chastity
of local pine,
sealed black,
without the sheen of polish
to soften the finality;
a new white sheet
at the bottom for a bed,
a prop for the head,
a fitted cover
to shield my ugly face,
and I am ready
to be lowered to eternity,
with the monks chanting
glad hosannas,
dropping clumps
of Stearns County,
pebbles of joy,

eight feet down,
drumming on my box,
thumping on my boards,
a staccato at the end.

If you return some day,
you can find my place
toward the top,
just before the hill
runs out of space,
as though I died
in a December hurry
—late again—
before the ground
gave out.

It is a comfortable place
to rest, if you must
speak of comfort
—your word, not mine—
I could mention
the view of the lake
beneath the hill.
You cannot see forever,

but the chapel
across the waters
commands the further
wooded shore
where the dogwood
bends into the maples.

But this is thin soup,
my friend.
You cannot warm me
in my grave
with dried crusts,
after the revelers
have staggered
out the door;
nor with woods and lakes
however radiant,
though when I was with you
they claimed me,
fed my starvations.

But if you pass this way
along the lake,
by the narrow of the road,

as the ground rises to a swell,
and wonder what keeps
young blood here
till they drop,
stop just before the gate,
look up the hill.
See the raw cross,
accusing and salvaging,
black against the sky.
Beneath the marshal of headstones
—our Omaha beach—
the gelded lilies of the field,
who toiled in song,
spun in penitence,
fighting with me,
for me, against me,
but gathered in praise,
dwelling in unity.

Man, don't ask me
why they stay.

COMPLINE

("No search for God is in vain." Bernard of Clairvaux)

One last exhausted
word of praise.
In starts and spurts,
against all temporality
and the pillage of the day,
I hunted you, Lord,
in the subtexts of my lean life,
in all the echoes of your presence,
but my heart is not ready,
my heart is not ready.
My body does not pine for you
as a dry weary land without water.
I have not conquered the noonday devil.

But I gather up the jumble of the day:
the tangled prayers, the angry word,
the walk I took to grasp the silence,
the class I taught to Visigoths and Ostrogoths,
the dissembled concession,
the carmelized insult,
the undifferentiated sameness of the hours.

I gather up my swampy fragments left over
as my day's doxology.

Two things do I know;
To one thing my heart clings:
One does not search for God in vain,
even if not found.

THE MONASTIC CEMETERY

("I have lived a failure." Bernard of Clairvaux,
On the Song of Songs, 20)

This is the Valley of the Fallen
on a hill. A temporary home
for the rest of available time,

a way station, permanently on loan,
for all the failures who failed
to keep the simplicities we vowed.

No grand betrayals
—we lacked the impudent will—
we died of small treasons.

We saunter down Mount Carmel,
come to the fork in the road,
take both to the left.

The coffins like trophies
beneath the great black cross.
"I will never take back my love."

FROM MONASTERY TO CEMETERY:
ST. MICHELE, VENICE

So now they dig graves for their mothers,
weep for their sons where once
the cells of monks in godly order stood,
relentless praise burned like incense;
that affront to TV manhood,
the swaggarts of Venice vowed their lives
like pouring purest water on the ground.
No lutes, no masks, no regattas down
the Grand Canal, but Vesper bells,
processional chants to the monastic choir,
among the gargoyles murmurs of glory
to come, to bed with a cold rosary.
A far different song for a far different land.

Giuseppe Musco and wife Rosa stare
from enamel portraits on the abbot's wall.
Paper roses on the prior's floor.
Beneath the cloister walk the rubble of the gone;
a monotony of crosses in the Lady Chapel.
No matter. No desecration among the dead.
Celibate bones, married bones,
one compost choir expects the resurrection.
Femur and fibula will waltz. Once more
the island of the dead is the city of praise.

THE MONKS OF ST. JOHN'S
FILE IN FOR PRAYER

In we shuffle, hooded amplitudes,
scapulared brooms, a stray earring, skin-heads
and flowing locks, blind in one eye,
hooked-nosed, handsome as a prince
(and knows it), a five-thumbed organist,
an acolyte who sings in quarter tones,
one slightly swollen keeper of the bees,
the carpenter minus a finger here and there,
our pre-senile writing deathless verse,
a stranded sailor, a Cassian scholar,
the artist suffering the visually
illiterate and indignities unnamed,
two determined liturgists. In a word,
eager purity and weary virtue.
Last of all, the Lord Abbot, early old
(shepherding the saints is like herding cats).
These chariots and steeds of Israel
make a black progress into church.
A rumble of monks bows low and offers praise
to the High God of Gods who is faithful forever.

PAUPERIZING

THE

COPTIC LEXICON

MILLENNIUM 2000

From three nines
I arrive at three zeros.
The airports are empty,
Times Square is full.

No one can say
it took me unawares;
even the stones
whispered apocalypse.

Still I am caught,
stranded on a one-way street,
disenfranchised by my own
uncertainty principle.

The door of '99
is still ajar,
for I have left
unwilling, unready,

—to tell the truth—
pushed from behind,
really Shanghaied,
gang pressed.

But now I'm here,
I think I'll stay
awhile to deconstruct
the future.

THE MABON MADONNA

(For the statue of Mary with the boy Jesus in the Saint John's Abbey Church, a bequest by Mary Frost Mabon)

Wisdom reigns upon a wooden throne
with eyes alone for tribal mysteries,
the Master lad upon her lap, bone
and sinews hers, now teaching with expertise
in the temple near the hill. She gives no decree,
has no answers she could put in speech.
God's Mother, Seat of Wisdom, does not see.
She walks with one candle, worrying each
adolescent triumph, teenage stumble,
still ignorant of the large design.
But the prophecy with thorns is there, the rumble
of falling and rising. She fears the sign.

Madonna, chewed by termites, with damaged hand,
you teach us how to kneel before we understand.

FATIMA YSIF BEARS A SON

My water broke as I,
a Moslem in a Catholic land,
was crossing the frantic Corso.
I leaned my great protruding selves
against the monument to Garibaldi,
my amniotic clothes clinging to our skin.

A black in a crowded bus with wet pants?
I still had time.
I began to walk along the road.
The terror fell at the four-mile mark,
as melt-down rants against
the wave on wave of inland pain.
I strain to lie upon the concrete curbing
where I will have a roadside baby.

Ladies pushing grocery carts pause,
rearrange their curls,
walk away.
A boy points, "Look what that nigger's doing!"

The garbage men park the truck to collect
the decay of our humanity
and stay to see the spectacle
in living color.

Not unobserved but unassisted,
I bear my son,
tear away my skirt
for swaddling cloth.

—Naples does not stir.
Vesuvius is silent.—

PASSOVER IN JERUSALEM

Even if there is no paradise,
even if no reward is waiting,
even . . . . even if Allah frowns,
the line is endlessly long.

Ayat swings down the street
after school, shouldering rage
in her bag of books to the guard
patrolling the market door.

A teen-age girl in slacks
pushing through the shopping
rush, racing to beat
the sun signaling the sabbath,

buying wine and matzoth
to eat with lamb and bitter
herbs, standing, remembering:
Egypt: more bricks, less straw.

Innocence yanks the ripcord,
a roar Masada hears: a thousand
suicides, resisting Roman
swords of an occupying army.

At Passover table Jacob
Raboniwitz asks his youngest
boy: "Why is this day
unlike any other day?"

IN DEFENSE OF PURITY

No visit to the mosque but to go-go bars
before they left for Boston and for death.

They drank to Allah and the prophet's health,
lifted five to zeal and righteousness,

a boasting banquet of rum and vodka,
three hours of toasts in wasted Arabic.

They had learned to fly modo Americano,
balked to pay the pilots' bill,

but what's a bar tab among friends.
On a vacant stool they abandoned their Koran.

MARICIA FROM POLAND

At four she wonders
where God lives
on Mondays,
and if it's cold
and snows in heaven?
Who cooks
God's steaks,
mops the floor,
makes the bed?
Does God have a belly-button,
eat turnips?
Does God bite?

THE PEARS OF ST. AUGUSTINE

("I stole, having joy in the theft."
Augustine, Confessions Book 2)

They were lousy pears,
blotched, chalky,
not worth stealing,
but heavy with delicious guilt.

The pear tree stood
in the middle of the garden,
surrounded by a wall,
guarded only by the night.

My gang sporting
up and down the avenues,
casing Babylon,
muscle stalking joy,

climbing the high gate,
shaking the forbidden tree,
the fruit rolling like soft dice
upon the evening grass.

We took one bite
(truly, lousy pears,
not worth stealing)
and threw them to the pigs.

But oh, the guilt,
the delicious guilt,
like the pure flame
of pure cussedness.

GOD IS NOT A PROBLEM

("A problem is something which I meet,
which I find complete before me."
Gabriel Marcel, The Mystery of Being)

God is not a problem
I need to solve, not an
algebraic polynomial equation
I find complete before me,

with positive and negative numbers
I can add, subtract, multiply.
God is not a fortress
I can lay siege to and reduce.

God is not a confusion
I can place in order by my logic.
God's boundaries cannot be set,
like marking trees to fell.

God is the presence in which
I live, where the line between
what is in me and what
before me is real, but only God

can draw it. God is the mystery
I meet on the street, but cannot
lay ahold of from the outside,
for God is my situation,

the condition I cannot stand
beyond, cannot view from a distance,
the presence I cannot make an object,
only enter on my knees.

DEATH IS FOR DUMMIES

("It is dumb to die. It is for squares." Timothy O'Leary)

Dam the rivers,
dynamite the clock,
burn the calendar,
melt down the bells.

Stop the measure
of movement,
carpe diem,
now is forever.

Tim, you're right.
If sensation is divinity,
if the palpitation is the ultimate,
it is dumb to die.

Do not allow
the glory of the glands
to lose their deity.
It's dumb to die.

You have friends, Tim,
priests of the senses
in the daffodil cathedral
chanting in the same mode.

"If the crowd, the host,
of golden daffodils,"
is as much of joy
as we shall have,

if "the greatest poverty
is not to live
in the physical world,"
then we're squares.

But Timothy, my boy,
it's a tattered tale you tell.
Wordsworth and Stevens
bet on blossoms and lost.

They sang and made
the icons weep.
No lie this,
but truth cut short.

Their chant falters,
the dancers tire,
red paint chips,
peacocks cry and die.

Seize the day,
the pledge of sense,
let it shout the forever
no one can tell.

Dying is for smarties.

DAKOTA SAMARI AT FOURTEEN

A foot of tumbled crisp geometries, snow's
white wisdom, lies soft across
Dad's new Ford waiting to be smashed.

Who of you at fourteen has not jingled
the mystic keys in a pocket of dirty jeans,
the long desired spurs of the unneeded shave.

The key rages the motor into furious life,
the car lurching through the swirl, a Samari
on a steed of steel for fifty feet of freedom,

shirring off the fender on Ruben Krebsbach's
car tethered just ahead. I was suckled
by wolves, ran with the pack. But I quake.

How tell the father of eight Apaches,
hot for the road and pieces of the world,
how tell of his fenderless pride and live?

"Son, it was your turn to wreck the car."

THE BIRTH OF ISAAC

At eighteen, a Greek god,
I strode upon the earth.
At high noon, a Masai warrior
with K-Mart spear,
full of temporary courage.
Clear of eye,
swift of foot,
newly greased and plastered hair,
I will live for ever.

At eighty-five, and looking for my mother,
I smell the crunch of my decay.
Face caved in,
de-toothed,
de-fanged,
I slant against my walker,
intimidated by Fiber One and prunes.
Gentle now because it pains to shout,
If it works, it hurts.

Dying is a tease,
but the great "I am" has spoken.
Death, like wizened Sara,
surprised by the surge of old delights,
giggles outside the tent
and lies in the face of God.
In mortality's wasteland womb
kicks new life.
The dying lady spreads her spider legs
and brings forth Isaac.

THE
MOMENT OF DECISION

Maiden Teresa West,
my eighth-grade teacher,
six-foot-one,
jaw assertive,
resolute of step,

eyes without eyelids,
is said to have
smiled once
(her first student,
Julius Caesar),

towering down
the aisle of desks,
caught me passing
lovely notes
to lovely Mildred,

the superintendent's daughter,
who had opal eyes
only for Kermit Fadness
(farmer hulk
of wavy hair).

Defeated in love,
disgraced before the school,
banished to the Alcatraz
of the nearest cloakroom.
I will be a monk.

THE DEATH OF MY MOTHER

She had no pain now, after eight births
no regrets, except those balls of dust
beneath the bed. And in a hospital!
With a vagrant mop the maid had left
against the wall she made a frontal charge while
on her back: with a one-armed backhand she reached
below the bed and in a single swoop
she vanquished them; depleted, she rested now.
At three the children gathered for the end.
Her daughter at the foot, five sons
around her, and my father praying at her side,
she faded in and faded out. As my sister
came in focus, "Mary, stand up straight,"
she snapped.—On second thought, if pressed,
she admits to one regret in the closet:
"I will never wear my new yellow dress."
And she was gone.

THE DEATH OF MY FATHER

All those years of smoking—no
chewing—cigars; cancer's revenge chewed
away the lip and jaw; like a great ancient
redwood, gouged, torn, tall, doomed
he drank his meals, spiked his malted milk,
slept, watched the Dodgers lose, shouted
insults at the umpire—where did they get this bum?
cheered the Green Bay Packers, faulted
the Dallas Cowboys—remembered the splendor, now
spent, of a voice that made the angels weep.
—in his good years he could hit high C—
At the end he was sitting sideways on the bed,
the brow depleted, chin upon his chest,
bloodless flesh, eyes closed,
labored breath. As the doctor poked, pulled
and yawned, he heard the thinnest voice, wrested
from Dad's last reserves, "Am I keeping you up?"

A bony uric bull, de-horned, could not
swallow, tore away the affront of tubes:
"It's dying time."

FEATHER AND ROCK

(For *Sister Mary Anthony Wagner,* O.S.B.)

Miesville sent its wisdom North
to the prairie house of praise
where women read the Word of Truth
and drops of silence day unto day
wear away the edges of unrest.

She opens adoration like the still of shadows,
wearies tomes heavy with footnotes
to make an eager Rahner groan,
stirring the waters of deep desire,
the marriage of feather and rock.

She raps the knuckles of established disorder,
which scolds her back "You shall not pass."
Do not bet the family jewels on that.
All the wise remember: the Ides
of March have come—but not yet gone.

The beavers are bushed, the owls are asleep,
all night creatures are in bed,
the light still burns in 111;
no "i" is left undotted,
no "t" uncrossed, no soul unsaved.

AFTER ALL THE WORDS

After I have emptied out
my store of words, depleted
all usuable sounds,
in praising God's unsayable
glory,

wasted the Oxford Dictionary,
pauperized the Coptic Lexicon,
have no breath between my teeth,
wordless beauty I give back to
God.

POET: CAN YOU START AT SEVENTY-FIVE?

Eight years ago, at the age of seventy-five, as I was reading a poem in the *New Republic*, I said to myself, "I think I can do as well," and started to write poetry. Writing was by no means new to me. For forty-five years I had been publishing scholarly theological books and articles as a monk/theologian, writing systematic theology out of a dogmatic, abstract, highly authoritarian, text-bound tradition. Apart from the concrete language of the Scriptures, I needed to relate to conciliar decrees, papal encyclicals, episcopal pronouncements, all highly conceptual, content and meaning-oriented. This was not a good preparation for creative writing. Too much imagination in theological writing can bring you to the stake. Could a seventy-five-year old man shift to the less logical, more metaphorical, evocative mode and become a competent poet? Real competence was my goal. Immortality I leave to the gods.

Of course, becoming a poet is not a decision; poets are born, not made. Allen Tate told a meeting of a Memphis poetry club devoted to moonlight-and-magnolia verse: "Stop writing poetry. People cannot join a club and become poets; they must be poets to begin with." As Tate well knew, the world is full of aspiring poets, not all of whom one should encourage. For one thing, the field is crowded, very crowded. W. B. Yeats once told the membership of the Rhymers Club in London, which included Ernest Dowson, Lionel Johnson, Arthur Symons, and Oscar Wilde, "I don't know whether any of us will become great and famous, but I know one thing—there are too many of us."

Among the millions of scribblers, was I among the chosen? Should I take Tate's advice? I showed some of my first attempts to persons competent to know and was assured that I had the gift, though it was raw. I would need training.

The Gift and the Craft

A novice at seventy-five, I had special problems. Though I had the gift, I would need to acquire the skills in a comparatively short period of time. I needed to make literary decisions, and I would not even know what they were unless I studied the tradition, the poetry of the masters (Dante, Shakespeare, Dryden, Keats, Shelley, Dickinson, Hardy, Yeats, Pound, Eliot, Bishop, Stevens). These past six years I have been reading the canon of poetry, biographies, and literary criticism. Though still a poetic toddler, I now have some idea of where the traps are. I also know that imitation is the first death. I will have to find my own voice. The biographies have been especially helpful for seeing how poets relate to the tradition but avoid repetition of other poets' voices. What I can learn from them is how they arrived at decisions concerning their craft and still write a new language.

During this period I was writing poetry two full days a week while finishing some theological projects. From my brother monks I received mostly encouragement. Fr. Godfrey Diekmann, o.s.b. who died recently at ninety-four, told me: "Kilian, stop writing theology. You write great poetry. Write poetry." However, another senior monk sniffed: "Kilian has idle hands. He writes poetry." This was too good to miss, and I turned it into a poem, "Kilian Does Not Have Enough to Do."

Like most writers, I write about my immediate experience, which for me, as a monk of some fifty-five years, is seeking God in a monastery.

For me the central metaphor of this monastic experience is Jacob wrestling with what appears to be an angel, but, in fact, is God, as recounted in Genesis 32:22-32. In the narrative Jacob is winning the match, but God cheats by a blow to his hip. As a sign of Jacob's victory, God changes his name to Israel "because you have striven with God and with humans and have prevailed." Jacob/Israel walks away from the encounter victorious, but limping. To a large extent my poetry, personal but not private, is about this sweaty wrestling with God, coping with the discipline of the search for God—or waiting for God. Something I learned from my brother monks and praying the psalms.

My grade-school piano teacher, who is still alive, took a stern look at my poems and declared them too grim. I have taken the criticism seriously, but I think she expected my poetry to be more lyrical, more joyous. I have taken my poetic stance from two Old Testament theologians, Gerhard von Rad and Walter Brueggemann. These two biblical scholars showed me how those who encountered God were engaged in a mighty struggle contending with God. The biblical characters of Adam, Eve, Able, Abraham, Sara, and Deborah bear in their psyches the marks of both a new level of freedom and also remnants of a limp. Sometimes the limp comes from the conviction that God has cheated, played foul. Other times it comes from failed shortcuts I tried to take. After decades of monastic life, my battle scars are my trophies of triumphs and failures. And if I limp, I know I am limping in the right direction. That limp is what my piano teacher thought was grim.

I have a major advantage over other poets, especially religious poets. I am a trained theologian and therefore have at my command a body of technical, scholarly reflection not readily available to other poets. I write most of my poems on biblical characters or themes, frequently after I have worked through technical biblical commentaries. What is of interest to me is less dogmatic questions, more the experience of the Word of God. But I can mine that experience in scholarly commentaries. Both in my study and in praying the psalms, I learn about the struggle when God becomes history. I do not write pious verse or sentimental greeting-card poetry. My poems are not sermons, not spiritual conferences. But I have to admit that they come out of a spiritual discipline, out of the experience of stumbling toward God. This is a matter of great seriousness, which does not exclude the comic embedded in the biblical text.

Style, I am convinced, is not a decision, but flows from the structure of one's life and the manner in which one appropriates experience. As a monk, I come together with my fellow monks twenty-six times a week for liturgical prayer, made up mostly of psalms and scriptural readings. In addition I have about an hour of *lectio divina* daily, private reading of the Scriptures, but reading with the heart. Technically this is not spiritual reading, but praying the text of the Scripture as one reads. In liturgy, *lectio divina*, and in my contact with confreres, the people I work with and in the surrounding woods and lakes, I do my wrestling with God.

Out of this combination of structure and freedom I have evolved a style which is personal, using a great variety of stanzaic forms, with attention to meter but with considerable freedom, some rhyme, unornamented diction, some fractured surfaces, a combination of what Robert Lowell called "the raw" and "the cooked" with a proclivity for the cooked, categories he took over from Claude Levi-Strauss. I take heart at the freedom T. S. Eliot and Ezra Pound promoted in the modernist stream but also note that interest in form is a dimension of modernity. Both Eliot and Pound felt some aspects of modernity needed repair.

Though I write some free verse I have my qualms. Much of free verse seems lacking in skill—more precisely, discipline. William Carlos Williams called it "slopping around in *vers libre*," the very malaise Eliot and Pound thought needed repair because form, discipline, and technique have not been mastered. I do not look upon form as law but, rather, with Emily Dickinson, as etiquette. If I have learned them well, I will know how to unlearn them at the appropriate time.

Pondered or Struck

I found myself torn between those who contend that labor, study, and revision produce the finest passages, and those who say that the words should not sound too carefully pondered, that the poem should be "struck," like a splash from an expressionist painter, coming without understanding, "out of the wall," or in "sounds not chosen" in Wallace Stevens's words. Stéphane Mallarmé said, "poetry is language in a state of crisis," the words coming out of that break in consciousness. Yet in reading Mallarmé one has the impression of chiseled precision rather than a word that fell into awareness from unendurable tension. Marianne Moore was accused of "thinking" her poetry, and Eliot of being too conscious he was an artist. But there is another side. Stevens believed that poetry was a conscious activity, and that one need not wait until one received an inspiration. Waiting on inspiration may leave you without poetry. You write when you can, as Stevens did as he walked to work at the Hartford Accident and Indemnity Company. Stevens, it was said, had such mastery he could write without inspiration.

Allen Tate suggested to his house guest Robert Lowell that a good poem has nothing to do with exalted feelings, or being moved by the spirit. It is simply a piece of craftsmanship. At the end of the day, after listening to the masters, I favor discipline and craft as I wait for that cry of surprise, the rapture of the deep. Still, poetry cannot be naked technique. For Hart Crane, a poem should be "a single, new word, never before spoken and impossible to actually enunciate" (a view he cribbed from Mallarmé). Emily Dickinson said she recognized true inspired poetry in two ways: if it made her whole body feel so cold no fire could make her ever feel warm; or if it made her feel that the top of her head had been taken off. If she is right, I have never read a true poem. And if losing one's skull is a sign of inspiration, I have yet to experience it.

I can think of moments when I came across an idea for a poem while reading scholarly theological works or when praying the psalms with my brother monks, but I can never recall a moment of real inspiration—if by that one means exaltation—except in the very process of composing. My first impulse comes from a Scripture reading while praying with the monks. At this level it is mostly conceptual. A great idea for a poem. The inspiration comes as I look at the technical biblical commentaries; or it can come after I begin to write, as I struggle to turn a theological proposition into experience. And then I do a considerable amount of revising, cutting. As I look at the manuscripts of the most elevated of the inspired, nineteenth-century Romantics, I note how carefully they have worked and reworked their poems. Perhaps I lack the capacity for rapture. But I have gasped.

Undoubtedly my attitude toward inspiration is related to the objectivism, some would say raging objectivism, of Roman Catholicism. The Church believes that truth not only sets one free, it is salvific. If one threatens truth, one endangers salvation. Therefore the Church has a magisterium, a teaching office, one of whose functions is to safeguard the orthodoxy of the faith and meaning. Both in reading and writing poetry I have had to school myself to go beyond meaning, beyond objectivism. I can sympathize with Billy Collins's dictum that high schools are the graveyard of poetry because literature teachers emphasize meaning. But I still wrestle with Mallarmé's contention that poetry is not made of ideas but of words. He was so sparing of even these that he left only one small volume. I struggle with Wallace Stevens's response to William Carlos Williams that meaning has little value because a poem is a structure of little blocks. Stevens did not intend to be obscure, but was unconcerned if not understood. When asked the meaning of one of his poems W. H. Auden replied, "your guess is as good as mine," and Marianne Moore said, "I knew what it meant when I wrote it." Meaning is my biggest obstacle, both when I read and write poetry. If a poem is not meant to mean but to be, then I have still a lot of painful unlearning to do. Catholic objectivism has me in a strangle hold. I know I need to break free for a while to wander in the intuitive, in the instinctive.

To Revise or Ship It

One writes poetry to record and communicate. I am now eighty-two, eight years down the road from my decision to become a competent poet. Though I see the monks of my age group dying, I still do not rush to print. To some extent I am torn. I remember the great advice of the Latin poet Horace (65–8 B.C.). When you compose a poem, he wrote in *Ars Poetica*, put it in the closet for nine years. If after that lapse of time you think it worthy, publish. Very likely I cannot afford the luxury of that kind of time. When I have done something really fine, my temptation is to ship it. But I resist. And the delay has almost always paid off. The caution about too much revising so that "the moment" is lost has thus far not been a problem. Walt Whitman seemed unaware that the moment would be lost; he was almost compulsive in his revising and redrafting *Leaves of Grass*. I do admire the spontaneity of the Beats, though it often appears as practiced spontaneity. Even though the Beats anathematized redrafting, one notes that their most important works were the result of considerable redrafting. T. S. Eliot advised the monk Thomas Merton to write less and revise more. Merton was devastated. I find Paul Valéry a good guide: a poem is never finished, just abandoned.

Unlike Gerard Manley Hopkins, for whom poetry was not very high on the agenda—he gave more time to composing forgettable music than to immortal poetry—after my monastic prayer and the common life, poetry is one of the most important things I do. Still, what can one reasonably hope for at eighty-two? Maturity is not legislated by years, but is guided by watchfulness and sensibility. I am no John Keats, but I find comforting that between his immature poetry of 1814–1815 and his mature poetry of 1818–1819 is a development of only four years. Few will be able to match this extraordinary development. Randall Jarrell noted that poets do not always get better with age. Paul Verlaine's great early poetry was followed by his later mediocre writing. Arthur Rimbaud wrote "Ophélie," one of his best poems, when he was fifteen, and when he renounced poetry at nineteen, he had radically impacted the poetry of the future in almost all languages. Shelley published his first book of poems at eighteen, Edna St. Vincent Millay wrote "Renascence" at nineteen. Though it was only published when he was twenty-three, Eliot wrote "The Love Song of J. Alfred Prufrock" at twenty-one. "Prufrock" is one of the great poems of the century. Jules Laforgue, indebted to Rimbaud, hated rhetoric and the proprieties of traditional poetry, wrote piquant, troubling, smudged verse, and at twenty-four published his only book of poems, *Complaintes*. He died at twenty-seven, but he influenced Pound, Eliot, Arthur Symons, and a host of others in significant ways through the Symbolist movement. He is still read. As for immortality, I remember W. H. Auden, looking back over decades of publishing, wondering if he could not at least salvage one poem to insure his memory in centuries to come.

At eighty-two I hear the clock ticking, but I take heart. At sixty-nine Thomas Hardy, after sixteen novels, turned to poetry, publishing twelve volumes, some poems written a few days before his death at eighty-eight. Robert Bridges published his very successful *The Testament of Beauty* at the age of eighty-two. One could argue William Carlos Williams wrote his finest poetry in his last years, in the ten years after paralyzing strokes. Randall Jarrell thought Wallace Stevens wrote his best poetry in the last two years of his life, in his mid-seventies. Gwendolyn Brooks was active up until her death at eighty-three, and Ruth Stone is still active now in her eighty-eighth year. David Wojahn thinks Czeslaw Milosz at ninety-three is doing some of his best writing. And who can excel Stanley Kunitz, producing superb poetry at ninety-eight? Courage, Kilian!

If age is not an obstacle, what can I do in a short time? Both T. S. Eliot and Richard Wilbur speak of poems taking years to write. Ezra Pound's *Cantos* span some fifty years. Obviously, I must find my models elsewhere. Keats wrote "Ode to a Nightingale," a poem of eighty lines, in a single morning. On another occasion, Keats and his friend Cowden Clark stayed up the whole night reading Chapman's translation of Homer. The next morning within two hours Keats finished his famous sonnet. Likewise Robert Frost, having written through the night composing "New Hampshire," sat down and dashed off "Stopping by

Woods on a Snowy Evening." Williams's "The Red Wheelbarrow" took two minutes to write. Even within the constraints of eighty-two years and counting, such writing takes on the character of the miraculous. And miracles are not mine to command.

A Tale of Two Drawers

With the clock running, I sought the mentoring of poet Tom McKeown, the founder of *The Wisconsin Review*, who helped me sharpen my diction. In June 2002 I attended a week-long advanced poetry workshop at Iowa City led by a masterful teacher, Michael Dennis Browne, from the University of Minnesota. After Iowa City I revised all of my poems. I keep on submitting them for publication, proceeding on the assumption that the first twenty rejection slips do not count. In my desk I have two drawers, one deep and one shallow. In the deep drawer I put my rejection slips, and in the shallow one my acceptances. In both there is plenty of room.

Randall Jarrell gives me comfort when he wrote, "All good poets write bad poetry." Even great poets and great poems find success elusive. During his lifetime Keats's poetry did not sell well. His first book was expected to cause a sensation, but passed unnoticed; the printing was small and never sold out. Wordsworth and Coleridge's *Lyrical Ballads*, perhaps the single most influential book of poetry in the history of English literature, was a financial failure. The printer remaindered the greater part of the five hundred printed. One publisher rejected Emily Dickinson's poetry because he thought it "queer," and another thought it unwise "to perpetuate" it. Though Hopkins was a Jesuit, the magazine *The Month*, edited by the Jesuits, rejected both "The Wreck of the Deutschland" and "The Loss of the Eurydice." The publisher of Hopkins's collected verse, edited by Robert

Bridges in 1918—twenty-nine years after the poet's death—had to wait ten years to sell all 750 copies of the first edition. Ezra Pound had to hound editor Harriet Monroe for six months before she agreed to publish Eliot's "Prufrock." William Carlos Williams had a particularly painful publishing history. At fifty-three, an established poet, he wanted to gather his scattered verse into one volume. His publisher reminded him that there were still 1,025 unsold copies of his previous books on their shelves. At fifty-five, his *Adam and Eve* sold only eight copies in a single year. His public reading at the Brooklyn Institute of Arts and Letters in 1936 was to a microscopic audience (though swelled by the presence of Marianne Moore and Elizabeth Bishop), and in the same year his *An Early Martyr* had sold only a handful of copies. Five years before his death, he had hardly begun reading his poetry at the National Institute for Arts and Letters when there were catcalls and boos from the audience. Wallace Stevens's first book *Harmonium* was roundly criticized for its abstract esotericism. His first year royalties came to $6.40 and the rest of the fifteen hundred copies were soon remaindered. But he was unrepentant, considering himself "the priest of the invisible." Poetry should be abstract in order to be more universal. Wounded, he withdrew, and licked his wounds in silence for about six years.

The problems of Marianne Moore were of a different order: double jeopardy. When she was in college her mother, a righteous Presbyterian matron, wrote instructing her how to fold a napkin, how to eat a roll. When she was an adult, her mother censored her poems, and even though her poems were accepted by other prestigious reviews, *The Yale Review*, *The New Republic*, and *The Atlantic Monthly* all rejected her poems. Her *Selected Poems*, with an introduction by T. S. Eliot, sold only twenty-eight copies prior to 1941, most of which she had bought herself.

The way of the poets is like the way of the monk. Commenting on "narrow the gate and hard the road that leads to life, and few there are who find it" (Matt 7:14), St. Benedict counsels young men not to be daunted by difficulties at the beginning. To overcome initial obstacles, some measure of self-promotion appears acceptable for poets, though Walt Whitman very likely went beyond the boundaries of the tolerable when he not only paid for the publication of the first edition of *Leaves of Grass*, but, leaving no stone unturned, wrote and planted three rave reviews, in one exclaiming "At last an American bard!," as though discovering for the first time a jewel of great price.

I had always thought self-publishing disreputable. Vulgar literary boosterism. If the poems could not make it on their own in the trade, they should remain unpublished. But I find distinguished names resorted to the vanity press. A. E. Housman's first book, *A Shropshire Lad*, was self-published. Ezra Pound, knowing that a poet should approach London, the literary capital of the English-speaking world, with a book under his arm, self-published his first book, *A Lume Spento,* in Venice in 1908, before he left for England. In the next year, William Carlos Williams paid for his first book of verse. Not to be outdone, John Gould Fletcher, following Pound to London, self-published five books of poetry. Among the others are Fenton Johnson, Marianne Moore, ee cummings, Robinson Jeffers, and A. R. Ammons.

But there is another possibility. One of my monastic brothers, Brother Placid Stuckenschneider, suggested that a printing business might be willing to print my poems as a Christmas promotional gift to its customers. The local printing firm, Park Press, agreed and I contributed my poems; Brother Frank Kacmarcik, an award-winning book designer, and

Father Francis Hoefgen, a photographer, produced a stunning volume, *Adam on the Lam*. The Park Press had its promotional copies, and I received some copies for my use.

But the beaten path to success seems to be through the little magazines. No publisher will look at a book manuscript of poems if the author has not established a name in these small literary journals. My success here is modest, and as a religious poet I have to expect special problems, as magazines serve their clientele. Perhaps I would have more success in breaking into print if my poetry were less personal, less about the personal struggle with God. Personal, but not private, poetry has a long history. After the death of his first wife, Emma, Thomas Hardy wrote poems of remorse for his neglect of her. The childless marriage had not been happy and Hardy blamed Emma. Ezra Pound's *Pisan Cantos*, written in prison, were deeply personal, even autobiographical. Many consider Robert Lowell the initiator of modern, more personal, confessional poetry. His *Life Studies* is an anatomy of his failed marriages with novelist Elizabeth Hardwick and Lady Caroline Blackwood. John Berryman's *Dream Songs* of 385 poems draw on his father's suicide when Berryman was eleven, and there are cries about the loss of meaning, when "things are going to pieces": alcoholism, broken relationships, multiple stays in the hospital, job insecurity. The very writing kept Berryman from being drowned in the chaos. His *Sonnets*, unpublished for twenty-seven years, are love poems about an extra-marital affair. Though these poets write about private matters, there is a formal public quality to their presentation.

My motto is "Dream big, but keep your expectations modest." When David Perkins published his *History of Modern Poetry* in 1976, he was able to say "none of the major poets of the twentieth century have been bestsellers." Edgar Lee Masters may not be a major poet, but his *Spoon River Anthology* (1915) was more widely read in his day than any other book of serious American verse. By 1923 the books of Rupert Brooke had sold three hundred thousand copies. The three books of poetry of poet Laureate Billy Collins published by the University of Pittsburgh have sold more than 105,000 copies. Even the support of the professional critics is not always decisive. A. E. Housman published his *Last Poems* in the same year as Eliot's *Waste Land* (1922) and it sold twenty-one thousand copies in the first three months. In spite of being savaged by the critics, it remains popular. Fortunately I have my monastic community behind me. It has given me major support in my late, late career. Abbot John Klassen, O.S.B., superior of my monastery, and Br. Dietrich Reinhart, O.S.B., the president of the university related to the monastery, were the ones who took the initiative to bring out this collection of my poems as the first of a series of publications issued by the St. John's University Press (in conjunction with the Liturgical Press).

At eighty-two, I will settle for modest success. A number of monks in my age group either have died or have moved into the retirement wing of the monastery, where there is twenty-four-hour nursing care. Intimations of mortality abound. I move toward the future with a certain dispatch, but not in panic as I contend with the infirmities of advancing years. Grandfather McDonnell lived until he was ninety-six, and great-grandmother McDonnell was one hundred and two when she was gathered to her mothers. I have no plans on going soon. Move over Stanley Kunitz.

This book is the first in a new series of the
Saint John's University Press, published at
the initiative of Brother Dietrich Reinhart,
O.S.B., President. It was produced by the
Liturgical Press with the encouragement of
Peter Dwyer, Director. The cover and the
text of *Swift, Lord, You Are Not* were
designed by Frank Kacmarcik, Obl.S.B., with
the assistance of David Manahan, O.S.B.
The cover photographs were supplied by
Francis Hoefgen, O.S.B. The text was set in
Zaph Chancery typefaces under the direction
of Colleen Stiller with Kathleen Zdroik as
the typesetter. Versa Press, Inc., printed the
book on Glatfelter Natural and bound it in
Nekoosa Feltweave Parchment.

The book was completed on the Feast of
Saint Thomas the Apostle, July 3, 2003.

This is an edition of 3,000 copies,
of which 375 are signed by the author.